origami
ANIMALS

Michael G. LaFosse

TUTTLE PUBLISHING
Tokyo • Rutland, Vermont • Singapore

Published in the United States in 2003 by Tuttle Publishing, an imprint of Periplus Editions (HK) Ltd., with editorial offices at 364 Innovation Drive, North Clarendon, VT 05759 USA.

ISBN-10: 0-8048-3527-6
ISBN-13: 978-0-8048-3527-5

Distributed by

North America, Latin America and Europe
Tuttle Publishing
364 Innovation Drive
North Clarendon, VT 05759-9436 USA
Tel: 1 (802) 773 8930
Fax: 1 (802) 773 6993
Email: info@tuttlepublishing.com
www.tuttlepublishing.com

Japan
Tuttle Publishing
Yaekari Building, 3rd Floor
5-4-12 Osaki, Shinagawaku
Tokyo 141-0032
Tel: (81) 3 5437 0171
Fax: (81) 3 5437 0755
Email: tuttle-sales@gol.com

Asia Pacific
Berkeley Books Pte. Ltd.
130 Joo Seng Road, #06-01
Singapore 368357
Tel: (65) 6280 1330
Fax: (65) 6280 6290
Email: inquiries@periplus.com.sg
www.periplus.com

First edition
10 09 08 07   9 8 7 6 5 4
Printed in Hong Kong

Diagrams by Michael G. LaFosse
Photographs by Richard L. Alexander
Design by Jill Feron

Contents

Origami Symbols Key

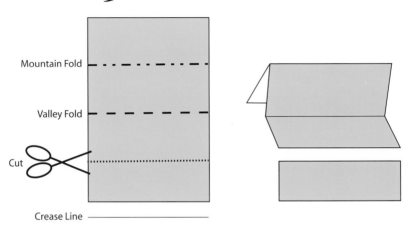

Mountain Fold

Valley Fold

Cut

Crease Line

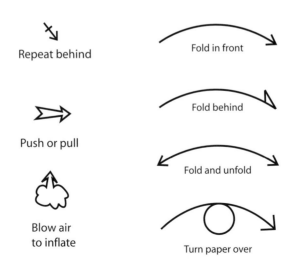

Repeat behind

Push or pull

Blow air
to inflate

Fold in front

Fold behind

Fold and unfold

Turn paper over

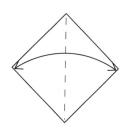

1. Fold in half, corner to corner. Unfold.

4. Mountain-fold in half.

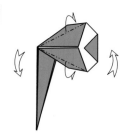

7. Mountain-fold edges behind the hood.

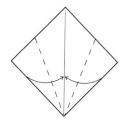

2. Fold edges to the crease to form a kite.

5. Fold top down.

8. Mountain- and valley-fold the tail.

3. Fold edges to the center. Fold down top corner.

6. Squash-fold to form the cobra's hood.

9. The finished Cobra.

Cobra

Designed by
Michael G.
LaFosse

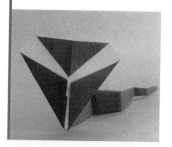

Seahorse

Designed by Michael G. LaFosse

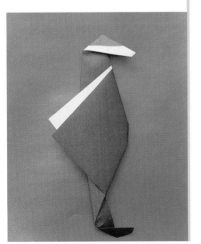

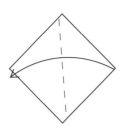

1. Fold in half. Do not match corners.

2. Fold over.

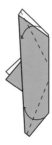

3. Fold top and bottom edges to the common, folded edge.

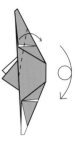

4. Fold top point over. Turn over.

5. Fold down the top point to form the head. Fold up the bottom point for the tail.

6. The finished Seahorse.

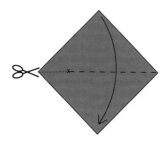

1. Cut one quarter in on the left side corner. Fold in half, top corner to bottom.

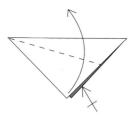

2. Fold up the bottom left edge. Repeat on the other side with the bottom right edge.

3. Your paper should look like this. Fold the bottom short edge up, matching the folded edge above it. Repeat behind.

4. Fold the tail corners at the cut end, one up and one down. Pinch the nose spike flat.

5. The finished Swordfish.

Swordfish

Designed by
Michael G.
LaFosse

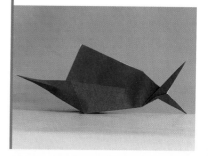

Whiskers the Cat

Designed by Michael G. LaFosse

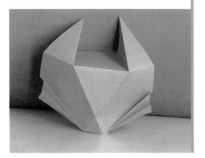

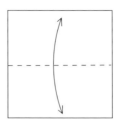

1. Fold in half, edge to edge. Unfold.

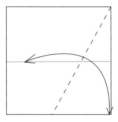

2. Fold the bottom right corner to the crease, making a neatly folded corner at the top right. Unfold.

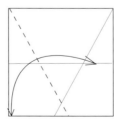

3. Fold the bottom left corner to the crease, making a neatly folded corner at the top left. Unfold.

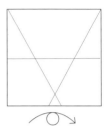

4. The crease pattern should look like this. Turn over.

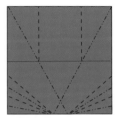

5. Mountain- and valley-fold the bottom corners, like a fan, to form the whiskers. Then, use the crease pattern to form the cat's head. Look carefully at the mountain and valley instructions.

6. The finished Whiskers the Cat.

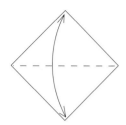

1. Fold in half, corner to corner. Unfold.

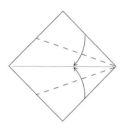

2. Fold the right edges to the crease.

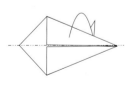

3. Mountain-fold in half.

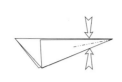

4. Pinch the narrow end to flatten the point. Make sure that an equal number of layers move in opposite directions: two towards you and two away.

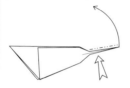

5. Push up the flattened point, mountain-folding it in half.

6. Inside-reverse-fold the tail down and inside-reverse-fold the head forward.

7. Inside-reverse-fold the tail up and outside-reverse-fold the head down.

8. Mountain-fold the back end in. Repeat behind. Mountain- and valley-fold the beak.

9. The finished Elsa's Swan.

Elsa's Swan

Designed by Elsa Chen & Michael G. LaFosse

Elephant Head

Designed by Michael G. LaFosse

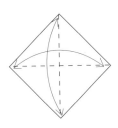

1. Fold in half, corner to corner both ways. Unfold.

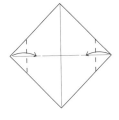

2. Fold in the left and the right corner, equally, less than one quarter each.

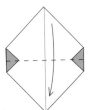

3. Fold in half, top to bottom.

4. Fold bottom edges in to the center crease.

5. Fold "ears" out.

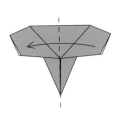

6. Fold in half.

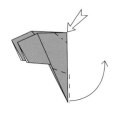

7. Inside-reverse-fold the top of the head. Outside-reverse-fold the trunk.

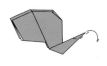

8. Outside-reverse-fold the tip of the trunk.

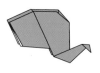

9. The finished Elephant Head.

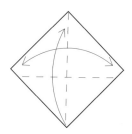

1. First, fold in half, left corner to right corner, and unfold. Fold up the bottom corner, but not all the way to the top.

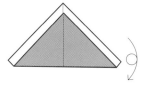

2. Your paper will look like this. Turn paper over, top to bottom.

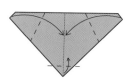

3. Fold the narrow edges of the ear paper to meet at the center crease. Fold up the bottom corner for a nose.

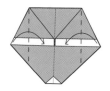

4. Fold in the side corners.

5. Mountain- and valley-fold the top and center line of the head. Open out the ears.

6. The finished Black Lab Head.

Black Lab Head

Designed by
Richard L.
Alexander

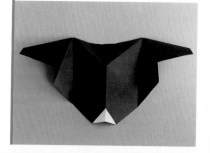

Cat Head

Creator unknown. Variation designed by Michael G. LaFosse

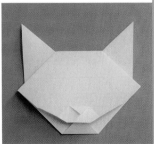

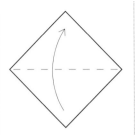

1. Fold in half, bottom corner to top.

2. Fold up the bottom corners, each touching the top corner.

3. Fold up the bottom corner, about one quarter.

4. Fold down the top corners, matching their folded edges to the outline of the bottom triangle.

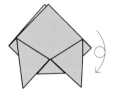

5. Turn over, top to bottom.

6. Fold up the bottom corner of the first layer.

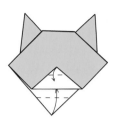

7. Fold up the bottom corner, tucking some of it under the folded edge. Fold down the top corner for a nose.

8. Mountain-fold the corners of the upper mouth under.

9. The finished Cat Head.

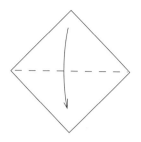

1. Fold in half, top corner to bottom corner.

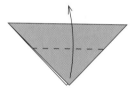

2. Fold up the bottom corner of the first layer above the top edge.

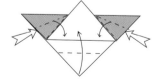

3. Squash-fold the side corners to make the ears. Fold up the bottom corner slightly above the folded edge in the middle of the paper.

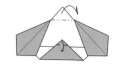

4. Mountain-fold down the top corner to the back of the head. Fold down the nose corner.

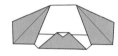

5. The finished Dog Head. What kind of dog did you make? Many variations are possible.

Dog Head

Designed by
Richard L.
Alexander

Fox Puppet

....

Traditional Asian design

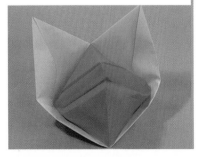

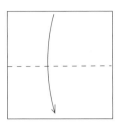

1. Fold in half, top edge to bottom.

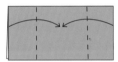

2. Fold in the left and right edges to meet in the middle.

3. Squash-fold the left and right sides.

4. Your paper should look like this. Turn over, left to right.

5. Fold in the sides and rotate.

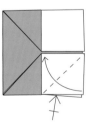

6. With your paper in this position, fold up the bottom corner. Repeat behind.

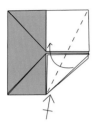

7. Fold in the bottom edge. Repeat behind.

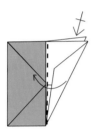

8. Fold the "ear" corner over. Repeat behind.

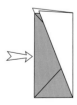

9. Push in the middle of the folded edge to form a mouth.

10. The finished Fox Puppet. Insert your thumb and fingers in the back and make the mouth open and close.

Fox Puppet

(continued)

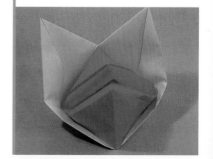

Duck

....

Traditional design

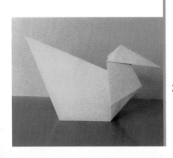

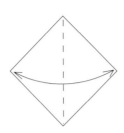

1. Fold in half, corner to corner, and unfold.

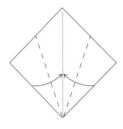

2. Fold edges to the center crease to make a kite.

3. Turn over.

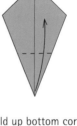

4. Fold up bottom corner.

5. Fold down corner to the middle of the bottom edge.

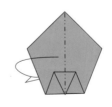

6. Mountain-fold in half.

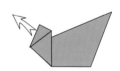

7. Pull up the head to shape the neck. Flatten well.

8. Pull up the beak. Flatten well.

9. The finished Duck.

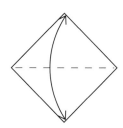

1. Fold in half, bottom corner to top corner. Unfold.

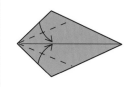

4. Fold in the left edges to the crease, making a diamond shape.

7. Inside-reverse-fold the end of each neck to form the beak of each duck.

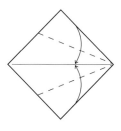

2. Fold the right edges to the center crease to make a kite.

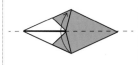

5. Fold in half, bottom corner to top.

8. Fold the baby duck over the back end of the mother duck.

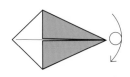

3. Turn over, top to bottom.

6. Inside-reverse-fold each end to form the neck of each duck.

9. Fold the back corner behind. A finished mother and baby duck.

Duck Family

Designed by Michael G. LaFosse

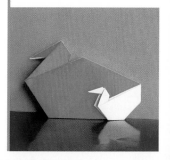

Macaw

Designed by Michael G. LaFosse

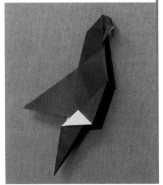

1. Fold in half, corner to corner, both ways. Unfold.

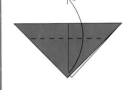

2. Fold up the bottom corner of the first layer. Look ahead to see how much paper to move.

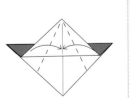

3. Fold the edges of the top triangle to meet at the center crease.

4. Your paper will look like this. Turn over.

5. First, fold down the top corner a little bit; then fold over again.

6. Fold in half.

7. Fold the bottom edge to the folded edge. Repeat behind. Pull out the head.

8. Fold out the corner of this layer. Repeat behind. Pull down.

9. The finished Macaw.

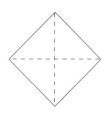

1. Fold in half, corner to corner, both ways.

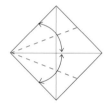

2. Fold two edges from the left side to meet at the crease. Unfold.

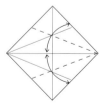

3. Fold two edges from the right side to meet at the crease. Unfold.

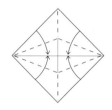

4. Fold all four edges to meet at the horizontal crease. Let the top and bottom corners fold in half.

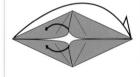

5. Fold in half, long corners to the right and short corners to the left.

6. Your paper should look like this.

7. Fold up the front tail point and fold down the back tail point.

8. The finished Fish. Move the tail fins apart to make the mouth open and close.

Fish

....

Traditional design

Unicorn Head

Designed by
Richard L.
Alexander

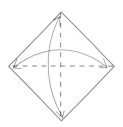

1. Fold in half, corner to corner, both ways. Unfold.

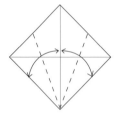

2. Fold two edges from the bottom to meet at the crease. Unfold.

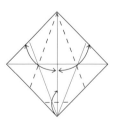

3. Fold two edges from the top to meet at the crease. Unfold. Fold up the bottom corner a little bit.

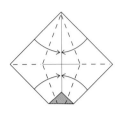

4. Fold all four edges to meet at the vertical crease. Let the left and right corners fold in half.

5. Fold in half, long corners to the bottom and short corners to the top.

6. Your paper should look like this. Outside-reverse-fold the top corners to form the ears.

7. Fold up the back corner to form the unicorn's horn.

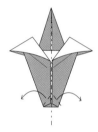

8. Fold out the nostrils. Mountain-fold the horn in half.

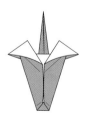

9. The finished Unicorn Head.

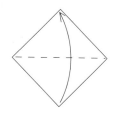

1. Fold in half, corner to corner.

2. Fold in half, corner to corner. Unfold.

3. Fold corners to meet at the center of the bottom edge.

4. Turn over.

5. Fold edges to meet in middle. Let corners come out from behind.

6. Your paper will look like this. Turn over.

7. Fold up the bottom edge.

8. Fold edge down to the bottom.

9. Turn over.

10. Fold corners over for eyes.

11. The finished Jumping Frog. Press on the back to make it jump!

Jumping Frog

Designed by Michael G. LaFosse

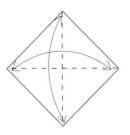

1. Fold in half, corner to corner, both ways. Unfold.

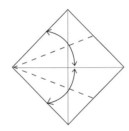

2. Fold two edges from the left to meet at the crease. Unfold.

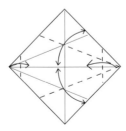

3. Fold two edges from the right to meet at the crease. Unfold. Fold in the left corner in a little bit. Fold the right corner in half way the middle of the paper.

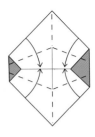

4. Fold all four edges to meet at the horizontal crease. Let the top and bottom corners fold in half.

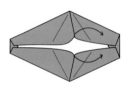

5. Fold the short corners to the right.

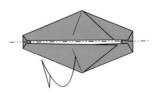

6. Your paper should look like this. Mountain-fold in half, bottom corner to top.

Seal

Designed by Michael G. LaFosse

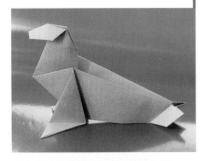

7. Inside-reverse-fold the left end to form the neck.

8. Inside-reverse-fold the head. Fold the front flippers to the front end. Valley-fold the right end up so that the bottom corner meets the slanted edge.

9. Fold up the ends of the front flippers to make the seal able to stand. Squash-fold the paper at the tail end.

10. Bend the paper at the tail end to center it. Inside-reverse-fold the back end to make it look forked.

11. The finished Seal.

Seal

....

(continued)

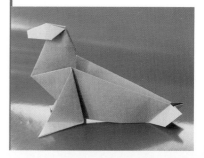

Owl

Designed by Michael G. LaFosse

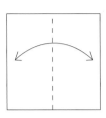

1. Fold in half, edge to edge. Unfold.

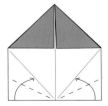

2. Fold all four corners to the center of the paper. Unfold the bottom two.

3. Fold the bottom edges up to the creases, left and right.

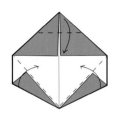

4. Fold down the top corner. Fold up the bottom edges.

5. Your paper should look like this. Turn over, left to right.

6. Fold in the left and right corners to meet at the center. Fold up the bottom corner (optional).

7. Turn over.

8. Fold over the two corners of paper that can be found under the beak—these will be the owl's eyes.

9. The finished Owl.

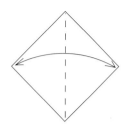

1. Fold in half, corner to corner. Unfold.

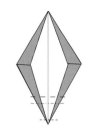

4. Fold up the nose point, then mountain- and valley-fold the head.

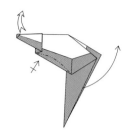

7. Inside-reverse-fold the tail up. Pull up the head paper. Mountain-fold an arched crease on each side, at the bottom edge.

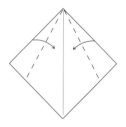

2. Fold in the top edges, but not all the way to the crease.

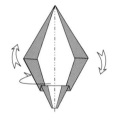

5. Mountain-fold in half. Rotate the paper, head to the left.

8. The finished Skunk.

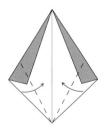

3. Fold in the bottom edges, the same amount as for the top.

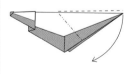

6. Inside-reverse-fold the right corner down. This will be the tail.

Skunk

Designed by
Michael G.
LaFosse

Carp

....

Designed by Michael G. LaFosse

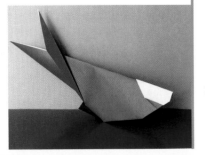

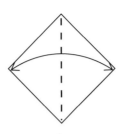

1. Fold in half, corner to corner. Unfold.

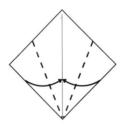

2. Fold bottom edges to the crease.

3. Fold corners out.

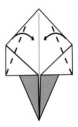

4. Fold sides in so that the upper edges are parallel to the center crease.

5. Cut bottom point up the middle. (A sheet of paper folded to this step is used to help make the shark.)

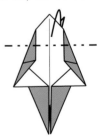

6. Mountain-fold top point behind.

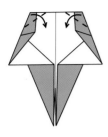

7. Fold down the top corners to round out the head.

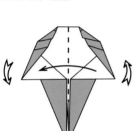

8. Fold in half and rotate sideways.

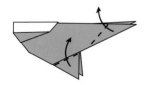

9. Fold up the fins and one tail point.

10. Curl the tail.

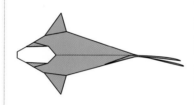

11. The finished Carp.

Carp

(continued)

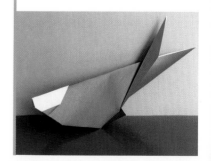

Shark

Designed by Michael G. LaFosse

This is a two-piece model. Fold one sheet of paper up to step 5 for the Carp.

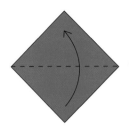

1. Fold the second piece of paper in half, corner to corner.

2. Fold down the upper right edge to the bottom edge. This is done only to the top layer of paper.

3. Mountain-fold in half.

4. Move "A" to the right while folding it in half.

5. Your paper will look like this. Rotate so that "A" is at the top.

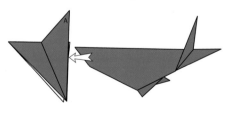

6. Slip the carp body between the fins.

7. Mountain- and valley-fold the fins to hold the carp body.

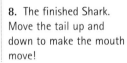

8. The finished Shark. Move the tail up and down to make the mouth move!

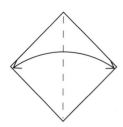

1. Fold in half, corner to corner. Unfold.

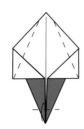

4. Fold sides in so that the upper edges are parallel to the center crease. Fold up the bottom point.

7. Fold the fins out on each side.

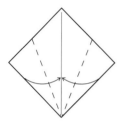

2. Fold bottom edges to the crease.

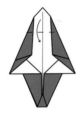

5. Fold down the top point.

8. The finished Whale.

Whale

Designed by
Michael G.
LaFosse

3. Fold corners out.

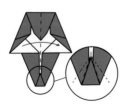

6. Mountain- and valley-fold the tail, then fold in half.

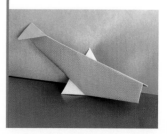

Horseshoe Crab

Designed by
Michael G.
LaFosse

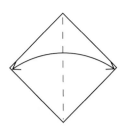

1. Fold in half, corner to corner. Unfold.

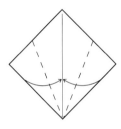

2. Fold bottom edges to the crease.

3. Fold corners out.

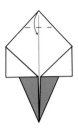

4. Fold top corner down.

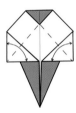

5. Valley-fold the two square corners in half, making the creases meet at the center where the top point touches the crease. Unfold.

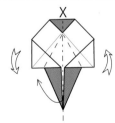

6. Inside-reverse-fold the tail while folding the front (X) in half.

X

7. Pull tail paper up, making the back wider.

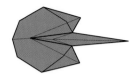

10. The finished Horseshoe Crab.

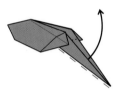

8. Inside-reverse-fold the tail up.

9. Mountain-fold bottom edges of the tail in.

Horseshoe
Crab

....

(continued)

Turtle

Designed by
Michael G.
LaFosse &
Richard L.
Alexander

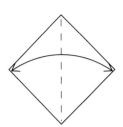

1. Fold in half, corner to corner. Unfold.

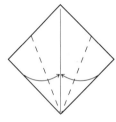

2. Fold bottom edges to the crease.

3. Fold corners out, but not all the way.

4. Fold down the top corner, then fold up bottom point.

5. Fold down the point.

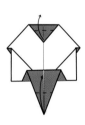

6. Fold up the top point, beyond the top edge. Fold up the bottom point.

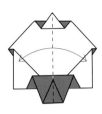

7. Fold in half and unfold.

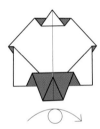

8. Turn over.

9. Fold corners over to make the eyes. The finished Turtle.

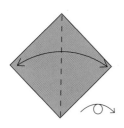

1. Begin with the black side up. Fold in half, corner to corner. Unfold and turn over.

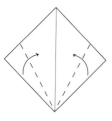

2. With the white side up, fold in the bottom edges, but not all the way to the crease.

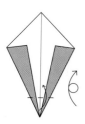

3. Fold up the bottom corner. Turn over, top to bottom.

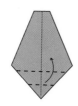

4. Fold up the bottom corner, over and over, to make the bottom edge flat and sturdy.

5. Fold bottom corners in.

6. Fold in half.

7. Pull up beak. Fold out wings.

8. The finished Simple Penguin.

Simple Penguin

Designed by Michael G. LaFosse

Dinosaur

Designed by Michael G. LaFosse

Fold each of two papers the same way and combine them at step nine.

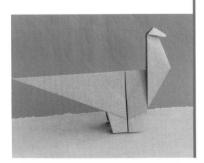

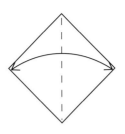

1. Fold in half, corner to corner. Unfold.

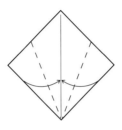

2. Fold bottom edges to the crease.

3. Fold corners out.

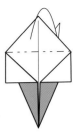

4. Mountain-fold top corner to the back.

5. Fold top and bottom corners to meet at the horizontal center.

6. Valley-fold top in half, allowing the back corner to come to the front.

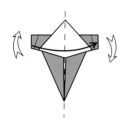

7. Fold in half.

x2

8. Your paper will look like this. You will need two.

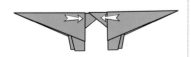

9. Fit two pieces together, one corner over the other.

10. Outside-reverse-fold the right corner up to make the neck.

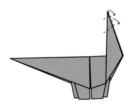

11. Outside-reverse-fold the top of the neck, over and over, to make the head.

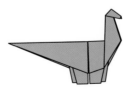

12. The finished Dinosaur.

Dinosaur

(continued)

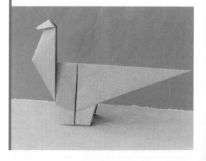

Hen

Designed by
Michael G.
LaFosse

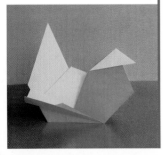

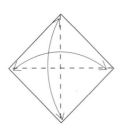

1. Fold in half, corner to corner, both ways. Unfold.

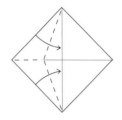

2. Fold the top and bottom left edges to the vertical crease. The left corner is folded in half.

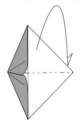

3. Mountain-fold in half.

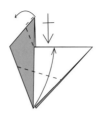

4. Outside-reverse-fold the top corner to make the beak. Fold up the wings on each side.

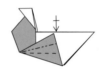

5. Mountain- and valley-fold the wings to make them fan-shaped.

6. Inside-reverse-fold the tail down.

7. Inside-reverse-fold the tail up.

8. Mountain-fold the back corners in.

9. The finished Hen.

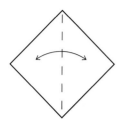

1. Fold in half, corner to corner. Unfold.

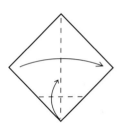

2. Fold up the bottom corner. Fold in half.

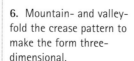

3. Fold the bottom edges up, matching the folded edges.

4. Fold over the top point.

5. Open the paper out.

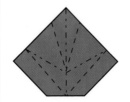

6. Mountain- and valley-fold the crease pattern to make the form three-dimensional.

7. The finished Sting Ray.

Sting Ray

Designed by
Richard L.
Alexander

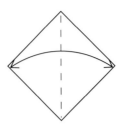

1. Fold in half, corner to corner. Unfold.

4. Your paper will look like this. Turn over.

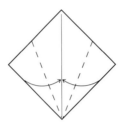

2. Fold bottom edges to the crease.

5. Fold down the top corners, making them meet at the crease.

Mouse

Designed by Michael G. LaFosse

3. Fold the top corner down, over and over.

6. Fold up the two corners for ears.

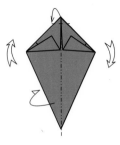

7. Fold top corner down for the nose. Mountain-fold in half and rotate, nose to the right.

10. Mountain-fold the bottom edges of the tail inside. Fold bottom corners in. Fold and unfold ears.

8. Inside-reverse-fold the left point down for the tail.

11. The finished Mouse.

Mouse

....

(continued)

9. Inside-reverse-fold the tail out to the left.

Bat

Designed by Michael G. LaFosse

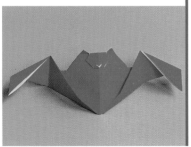

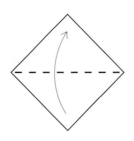

1. Fold in half, bottom corner to top corner.

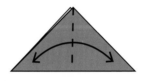

2. Fold in half, left corner to right corner. Unfold.

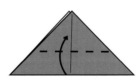

3. Fold up bottom edge, about one third.

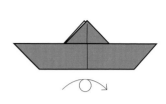

4. Turn over.

5. Fold up the left and right halves of the bottom edge to form the wings.

6. Fold down the outside corners of the wings.

7. Fold and unfold each wing in half.

8. Fold down the top corner to form the head.

9. Fold up the corner to make upper lip.

10. Fold down corner to make the nose.

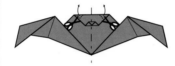

11. Cut on each side of the head. Fold up the ears.

12. The finished Bat.

Bat
....
(continued)

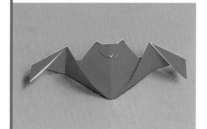

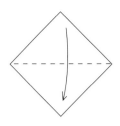

1. Fold in half, top corner to bottom corner.

Scorpion

Designed by
Michael G.
LaFosse

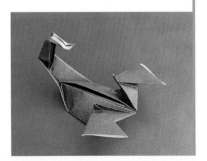

2. Fold in the left and right edges to meet in the middle.

3. Your paper will look like this. Turn over.

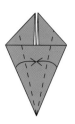

4. Fold in the left and right sides.

5. Turn over.

6. Fold down the top corners, one to the left and one to the right.

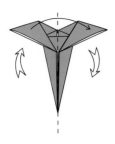

7. Fold in half and rotate.

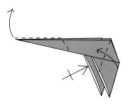

8. Outside-reverse-fold the tail. Fold back the claws.

9. Inside-reverse-fold the tail. Fold up the claws.

10. Inside-reverse-fold the tip of the tail. Fold up along the folded edge to raise the claws. Repeat behind.

11. The finished Scorpion.

Scorpion

(continued)

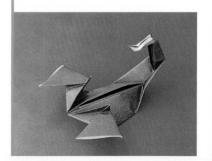

Bobbing Fox

....

Designed by Michael G. LaFosse

You will need two sheets of square paper for this project.

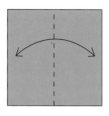

1. Fold in half, edge to edge. Unfold.

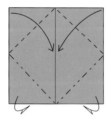

2. Fold the top corners to the center of the front and the bottom corners to the center of the back.

3. Your paper should look like this.

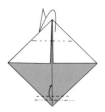

4. Fold the top corner to the center of the back. Mountain- and valley-fold the bottom corner for a nose.

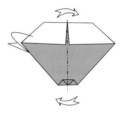

5. Mountain-fold in half. Rotate the nose to the left.

6. Pull up the top right corner while folding the bottom corner up. Repeat behind.

7. The completed head.

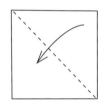

8. Fold a new sheet of paper in half, corner to corner.

9. Fold one corner over for a tail.

10. Balance the head on the top point. The finished Bobbing Fox!

Bobbing Fox

....

(continued)

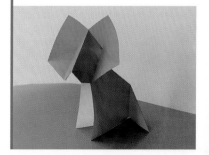

Pajarita (Little Bird)

Traditional Spanish design

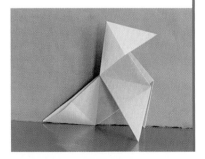

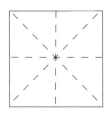

1. Valley-fold in half, corner to corner and edge to edge.

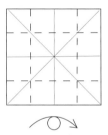

2. Fold and unfold each edge to the center. Turn over.

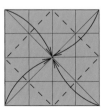

3. Fold all four corners to the center.

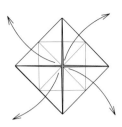

4. Unfold.

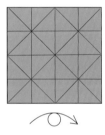

5. Your paper will look like this. Turn over.

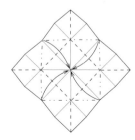

6. Using the crease pattern, bring the center of all four edges to meet at the middle of the paper. Let each corner fold in half.

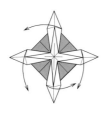

7. Fold each corner over: Top, to the left; bottom, to the right; left and right corners down.

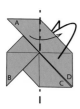

8. Mountain-fold in half, moving D to the left and letting A move to the right.

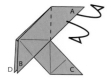

9. Turn point A inside-out.

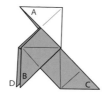

10. The finished Pajarita.

Pajarita (Little Bird)

(continued)

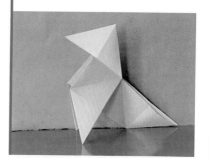

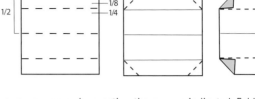

1. Prepare your paper by creating the creases indicated. Fold all four corners in and then fold over the top and bottom edges. You can experiment with different measurements and make many kinds of butterflies.

Alice's Butterfly

Designed by
Michael G. LaFosse
and named for
Alice Gray

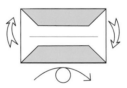

2. Your paper should look like this. Turn over.

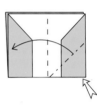

4. Squash-fold the right half to the front.

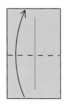

3. Fold in half, short edges together.

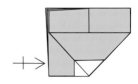

5. Repeat behind.

6. Fold up the bottom corner to the middle of the top. Unfold.

7. Bring both "Y" corners down.

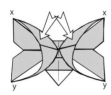

8. Squash-fold the left and right sides to form the wings.

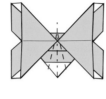

9. Mountain- and valley-fold the center to form the body.

10. The finished Alice's Butterfly.

Alice's
Butterfly

....

(continued)

Husky Pup

Designed by
Michael G.
LaFosse

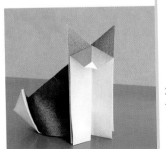

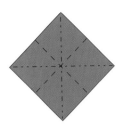

1. Begin colored side up. Mountain-fold, corner to corner each way, and valley-fold edge to edge each way.

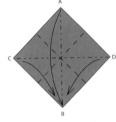

2. Fold on the existing creases to bring corners C, A and D down to B.

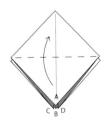

3. Fold up corner A to the top.

4. Turn the paper over, bottom to top.

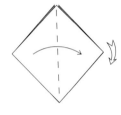

5. Fold in half, left to right and rotate.

6. Fold the set of right edges over.

7. Open these edges at the center and squash-fold the middle point down. Outside-reverse-fold the left corner for a tail.

8. The finished Husky Pup.

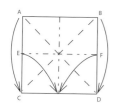

1. Make mountain folds, edge to edge, and valley folds, corner to corner, on the white side of the paper.

2. Mountain-fold the E and F edges, bringing A down to C and B down to D.

3. Inside-reverse-fold A and B.

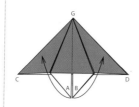

4. Inside-reverse-fold A and B up.

5. Fold in half.

6. Fold up the bottom corners, one on each side.

7. Fold over the top edges and squash-fold the center corner point. Rotate.

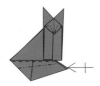

8. Mountain- and valley-fold the base edges on each size. Mountain-fold the nose to make it fox-like.

9. Center the front to face forward. The finished Anubis.

Anubis

Designed by Richard L. Alexander

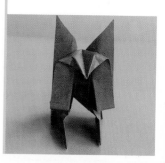

Phoenix

Designed by Michael G. LaFosse and Satoshi Kamiya

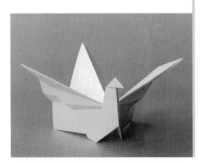

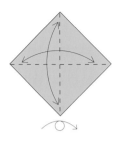

1. Valley-fold on the colored side, corner to corner both ways. Turn over.

4. Fold the bottom edges to meet at the crease. Unfold.

2. Valley-fold on the white side, edge to edge.

5. Fold the bottom corner of the top layer up, while folding X behind. Let the side edges fold in to form a diamond shape in front.

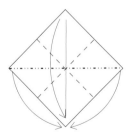

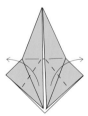

3. Bring all corners to meet at the bottom.

6. Fold bottom corners out to form the wings.

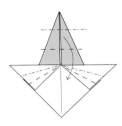

7. Mountain- and valley-fold each wing into a fan. Mountain- and valley-fold the top corner to form the neck and beak.

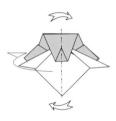

8. Mountain-fold in half.

9. Open out the wings.

10. The finished Phoenix.

Phoenix

(continued)

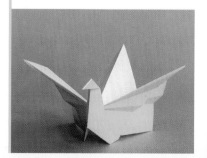

Flapping Bird

Traditional Japanese design

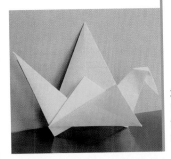

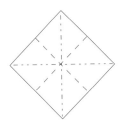

1. Make mountain folds, corner to corner, and valley folds, edge to edge, on the white side of the paper.

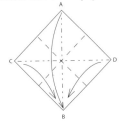

2. Mountain-fold the C and D corners, bringing A, C and D down to B.

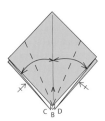

3. Your paper should look like this. Fold and unfold the bottom open edges to the crease. Repeat behind.

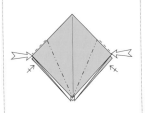

4. Push in the corners, following the creases from step three. Repeat behind.

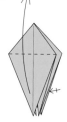

5. The front and back flaps should now be free. Fold up the front flap. Repeat behind.

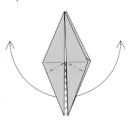

6. Inside-reverse-fold the bottom corners, one to the right and one to the left.

7. Inside-reverse-fold one corner for the beak. Fold down the wings.

8. The finished Flapping Bird. Hold the bottom front and pull the tail in and out to make the wings flap!

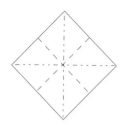

1. Make mountain folds, corner to corner, and valley folds, edge to edge, on the white side of the paper.

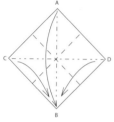

2. Mountain-fold the C and D corners, bringing A, C and D down to B.

3. Your paper should look like this. Fold and unfold the bottom open edges to the crease. Repeat behind.

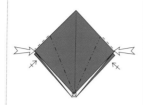

4. Push in the corners, following the creases from step three. Repeat behind.

5. Fold up the front flap. Repeat behind.

6. Fold in the bottom edges, two in the front and two in the back.

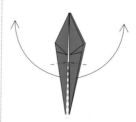

7. Inside-reverse-fold the bottom corners.

8. Inside-reverse-fold one corner for the beak. Fold down the wings.

9. The finished Crane.

Crane

....

Traditional Japanese design

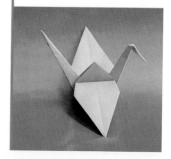

Frog

....

Traditional Japanese design

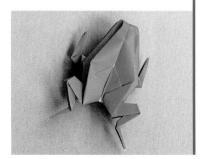

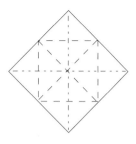

1. On the white side of the paper, make mountain folds, corner to corner, and valley folds, edge to edge. Valley-fold and unfold the four corners to the center.

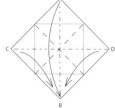

2. Mountain-fold the C and D corners, bringing A, C and D down to B.

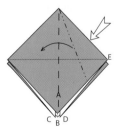

3. Lift corner E, open the layers and flatten it. Look ahead at step **4**.

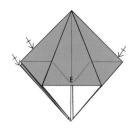

4. Repeat behind, and then with the two inside corners, turning the layers to reveal them.

5. Move the middle edge towards the top, while folding in the edges of the top layers. Repeat behind, and then with the two inside layers. Look ahead to step 6 for the shape.

6. Your paper should look like this.

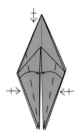

7. Fold the bottom left and the bottom right edges to the split. Repeat behind and with the middle layers.

8. Inside-reverse-fold, to form the front legs.

9. Turn over.

10. Inside-reverse-fold, to form the hind legs.

11. Make inside-reverse folds to form joints in the legs. Look at step 12 for the shape. Blow air into the frog to make it plump.

12. The finished Frog.

Frog

....

(continued)

Swallow

Traditional Japanese design

1. Make mountain folds, edge to edge, and valley folds, corner to corner, on the white side of the paper.

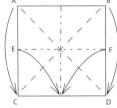

2. Mountain-fold the E and F edges, bringing A down to C and B down to D.

3. Fold B over A, equally.

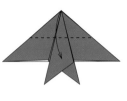

4. Fold down the top corner.

5. Fold the corner up above the top edge.

6. Turn over.

7. Fold in half.

8. Open.

9. The finished Swallow.

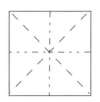

1. Make mountain folds, edge to edge, and valley folds, corner to corner, on the white side of the paper.

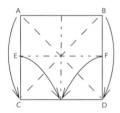

2. Mountain-fold the E and F edges, bringing A down to C and B down to D.

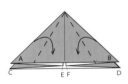

3. Fold A and B in at an angle but not to the center.

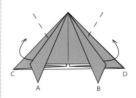

4. Fold up C and D, behind A and B. Look at step five for the shape.

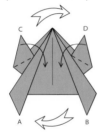

5. Fold C and D down. Rotate the mask, bottom up.

6. Mountain- and valley-fold the top corners for ears. Fold middle corners over for eyes. Mountain- and valley-fold bottom corner for a nose.

7. Mountain-fold the top corner to the back. Mountain-fold the sides of the face in, following the folded edges.

8. The finished Fox Mask.

Fox Mask

Designed by
Michael G.
LaFosse

Bunny Balloon

Traditional design

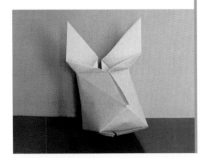

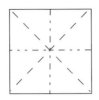

1. Make mountain folds, edge to edge, and valley folds, corner to corner, on the white side of the paper.

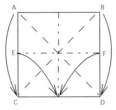

2. Mountain-fold the E and F edges, bringing A down to C and B down to D.

3. Fold A and B up to G.

4. Fold in the left and right front corners to meet at the center of the paper.

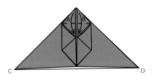

5. Fold down A and B.

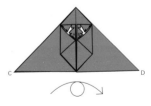

6. Tuck into pockets. Turn over.

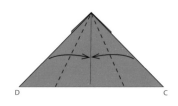

7. Fold edges to meet at the crease.

8. Fold points D and C out to the left and to the right, as far as possible.

9. Fold bottom corners to meet at the center of the paper.

10. Blow air into opening.

11. The finished Bunny Balloon.

Bunny Balloon

(continued)

1. Fold in half, edge to edge each way, to mark your paper with crossing creases.

Cardinal

Designed by Michael G. LaFosse

Use red and black papers, back to back. Begin with the black side up.

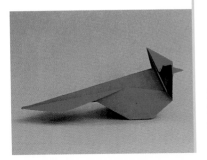

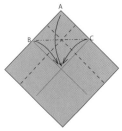

2. Fold the top edges to the crease lines and unfold. Fold the top corner to the center of the back and unfold. Use these mountain and valley creases to bring A, B and C together.

3. Your paper should look like this. Fold over the right corner at the top square.

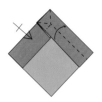

4. Fold the cut edge to the folded edge while mountain- and valley-folding the upper square area. Repeat on the other side.

5. Fold the top corner to the back, letting A move to the top.

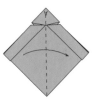

6. Fold in half.

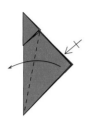

7. Fold right corner over. Repeat behind.

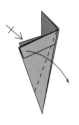

8. Fold corner down. Repeat behind.

9. Mountain-fold bottom edge inside. Repeat behind.

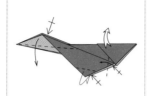

10. Fold tail papers down on each side. Pull up on the crest of the head, letting the paper in the neck fold up to show the black color. Fold under the bottom corners.

11. Fold up the bottom corner of the head. Unfold and repeat behind.

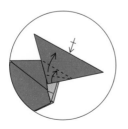

12. Fold the bottom right edge up to the crease then fold up again. Repeat behind.

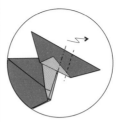

13. Mountain- and valley- fold the front corner to form the beak.

14. The finished Cardinal.

Cardinal

(continued)

Barking Dog Head

Designed by Michael G. LaFosse

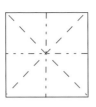

1. Make mountain folds, edge to edge, and valley folds, corner to corner, on the white side of the paper.

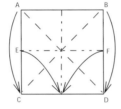

2. Mountain-fold the E and F edges, bringing A down to C and B down to D.

3. Fold B over to A.

4. Fold B up, moving the bottom edge to the right side of the triangle. Squash-fold the paper between points B and A. Repeat behind.

5. Your paper should look like this.

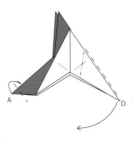

6. Inside-reverse-fold D to make the lower jaw. Outside-reverse-fold point A over for a nose.

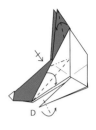

7. Fold in the tip of the lower jaw. Fold white edge down while folding ear in half (optional).

8. The finished Barking Dog Head. Pull the ears to make the mouth open and close!